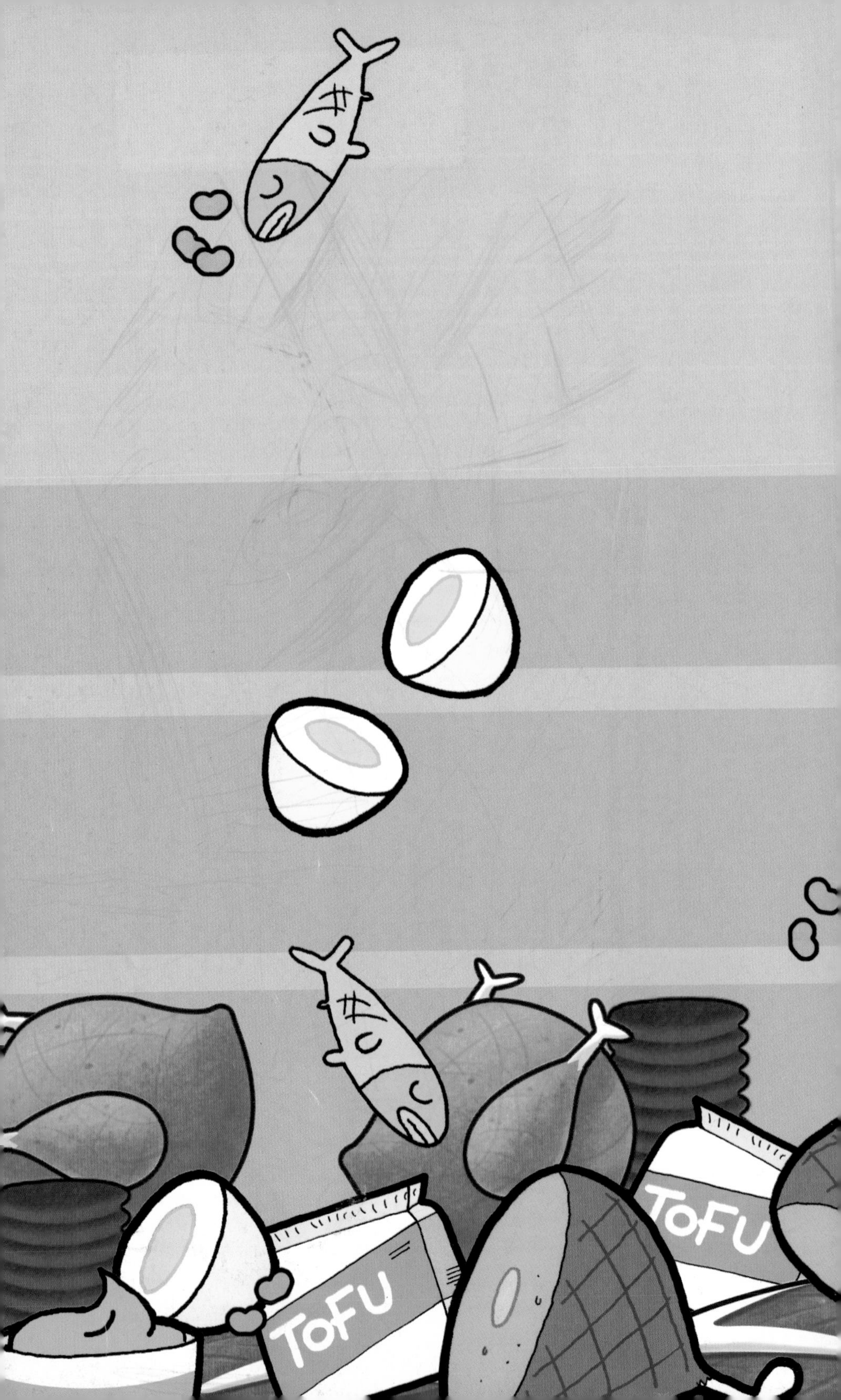
ToFU
ToFU

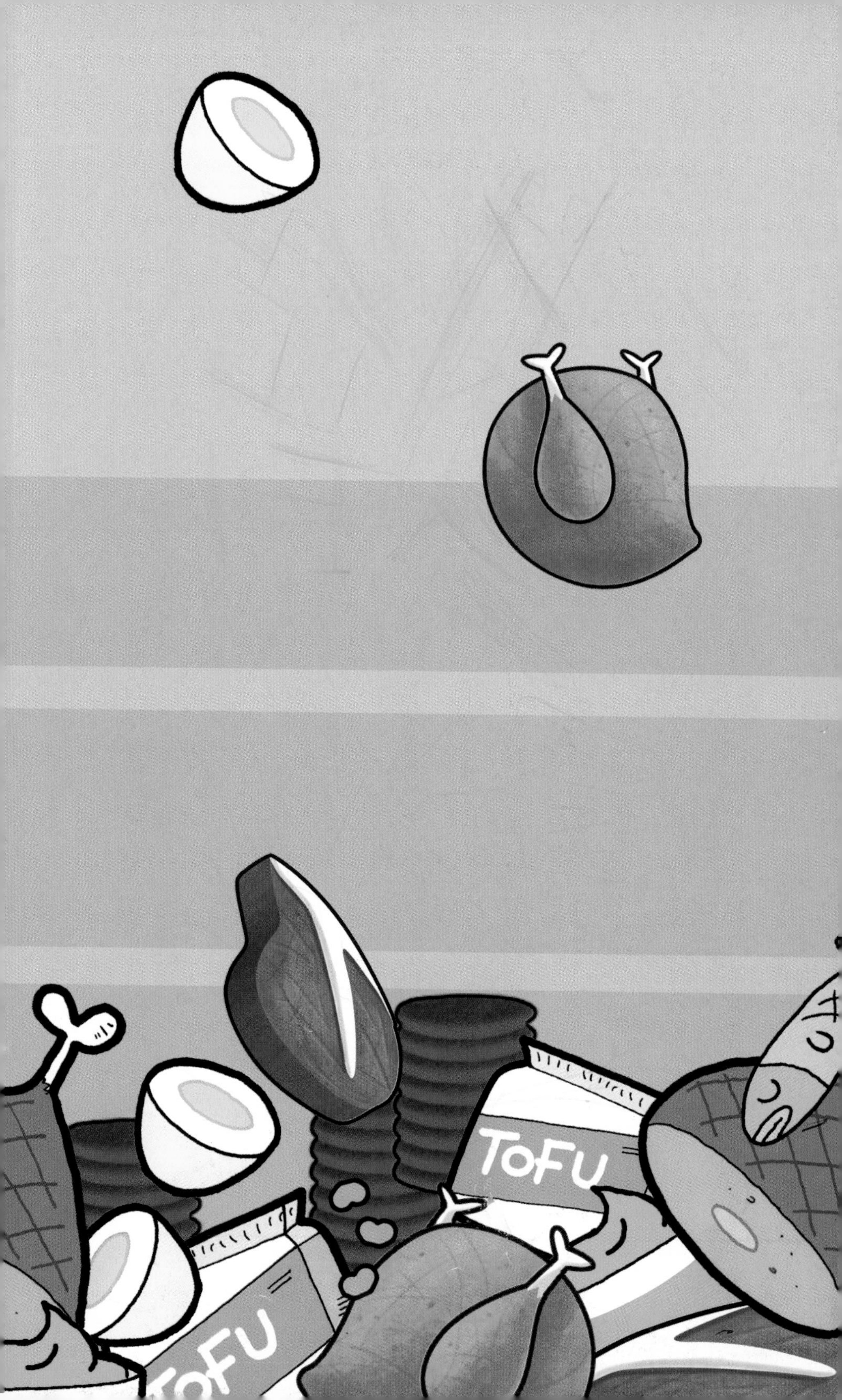
ToFU
ToFU

First Graphics

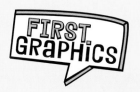

MyPlate and Healthy Eating

The Powerful Protein Group

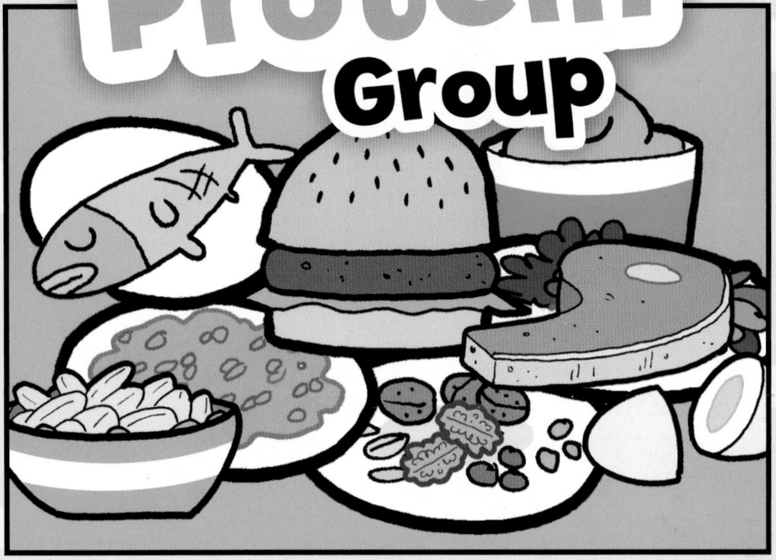

By Sally Lee

Illustrated by Gary Swift

Consultant: Amy Lusk, MS, RD, LD
Registered Dietitian
Nationwide Children's Hospital, Columbus, Ohio

CAPSTONE PRESS
a capstone imprint

First Graphics are published by Capstone Press,
151 Good Counsel Drive, P.O. Box 669, Mankato, Minnesota 56002.
www.capstonepub.com

 Books published by Capstone Press are manufactured with paper containing at least 10 percent post-consumer waste.

Library of Congress Cataloging-in-Publication Data
Lee, Sally.
  The Powerful Protein Group / by Sally Lee ; illustrated by Gary Swift.
    p. cm.—(First graphics. MyPlate and healthy eating)
  Summary: "Simple text and illustrations present MyPlate and the protein foods
group, the foods in this group, and examples of healthy eating choices"
—Provided by publisher.
  Includes bibliographical references and index.
  ISBN 978-1-4296-6091-4 (library binding)
  ISBN 978-1-4296-7164-4 (paperback)
  1. Meat—Juvenile literature. 2. Beans—Juvenile literature. I. Swift, Gary. II.
Title. III. Series.

  TX373.L44 2012
  641.6'6—dc22

                          2011002448

Editorial Credits
Lori Shores, editor; Juliette Peters, designer; Nathan Gassman,
    art director; Eric Manske, production specialist

Image Credits
USDA/MyPlate.com 4, 5 (MyPlate icon)

Serving sizes are based on recommendations for children ages 4 through 8.

Printed in the United States of America in Stevens Point, Wisconsin.
032011   006240F11

Table of Contents

The Protein Foods Group

Your body needs many kinds of foods each day.

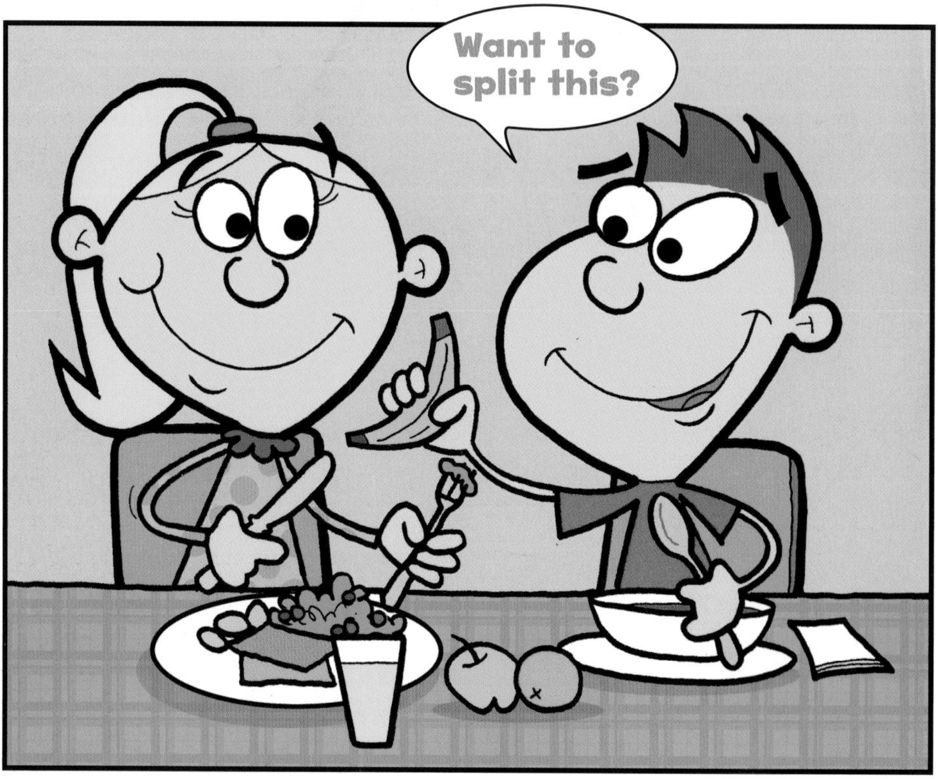
Want to
split this?

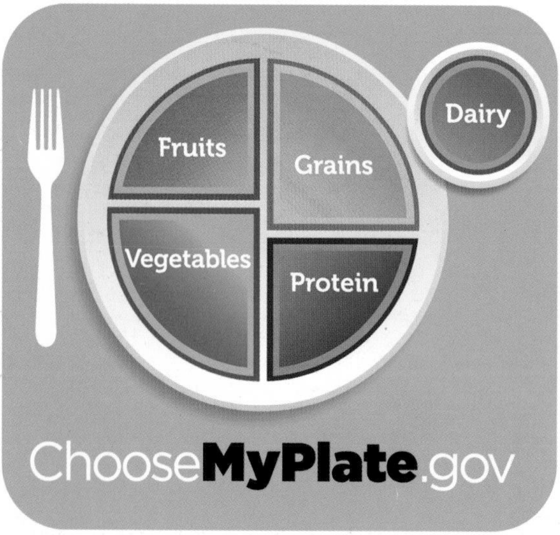
Fruits
Grains
Dairy
Vegetables
Protein
ChooseMyPlate.gov

MyPlate includes all five food groups. It is a guide to help you choose a healthy mix of foods.

You need more food from some groups and less from others.

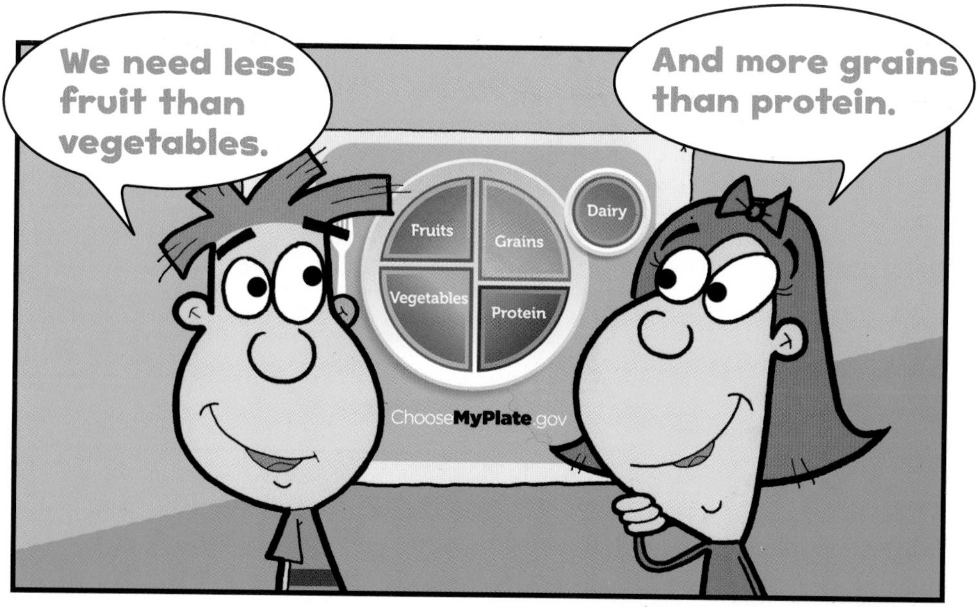
We need less fruit than vegetables.
And more grains than protein.
Dairy
Fruits
Grains
Vegetables
Protein
ChooseMyPlate.gov

Eating foods from each group gives your body what it needs.

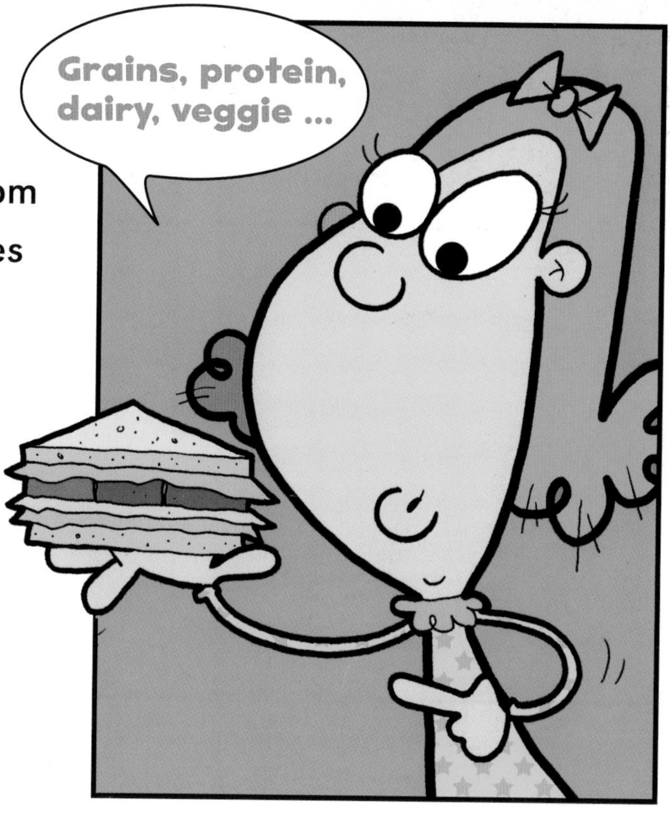
Grains, protein, dairy, veggie ...

The protein foods group includes meat and other foods with protein.

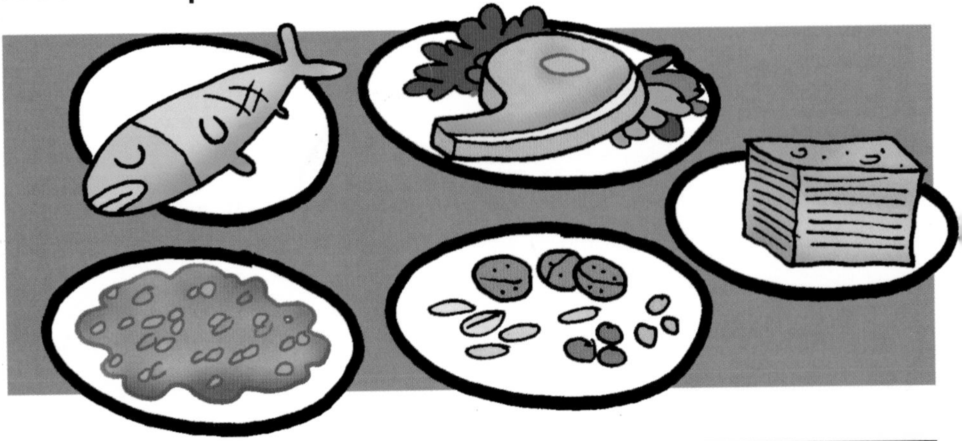

Beef, pork, chicken, and fish are in this group.

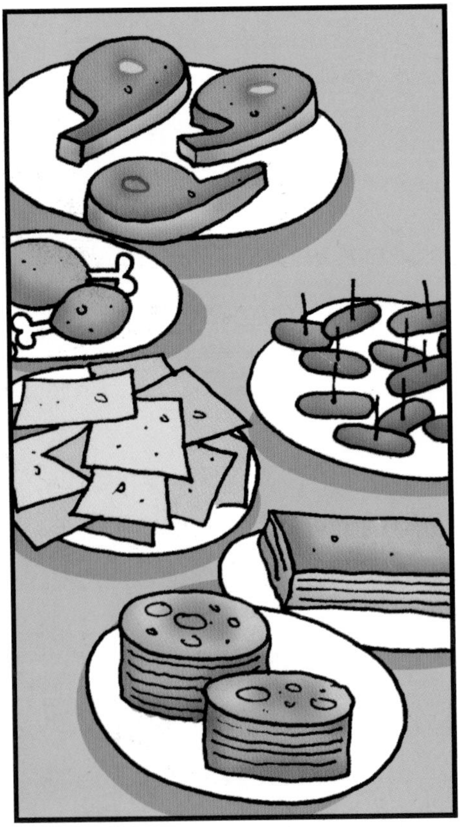

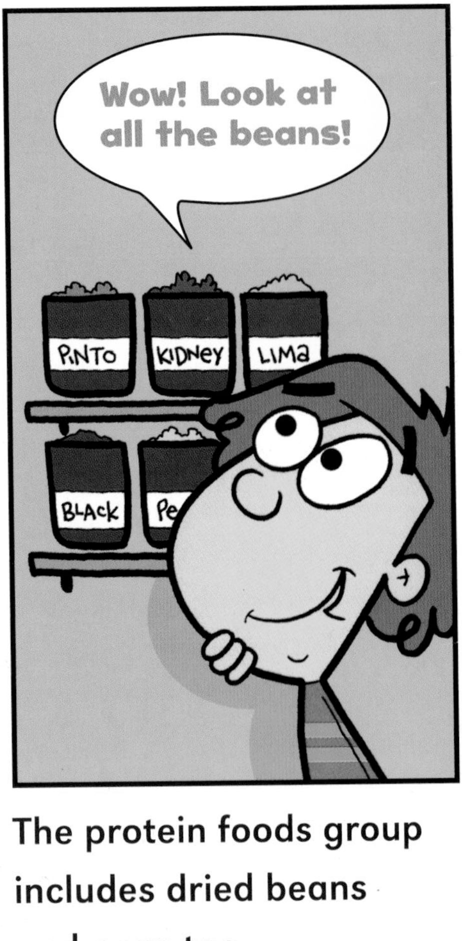
Wow! Look at all the beans!
PINTO
KIDNEY
LIMA
BLACK

The protein foods group includes dried beans and peas too.

Eggs and tofu are also sources of protein.

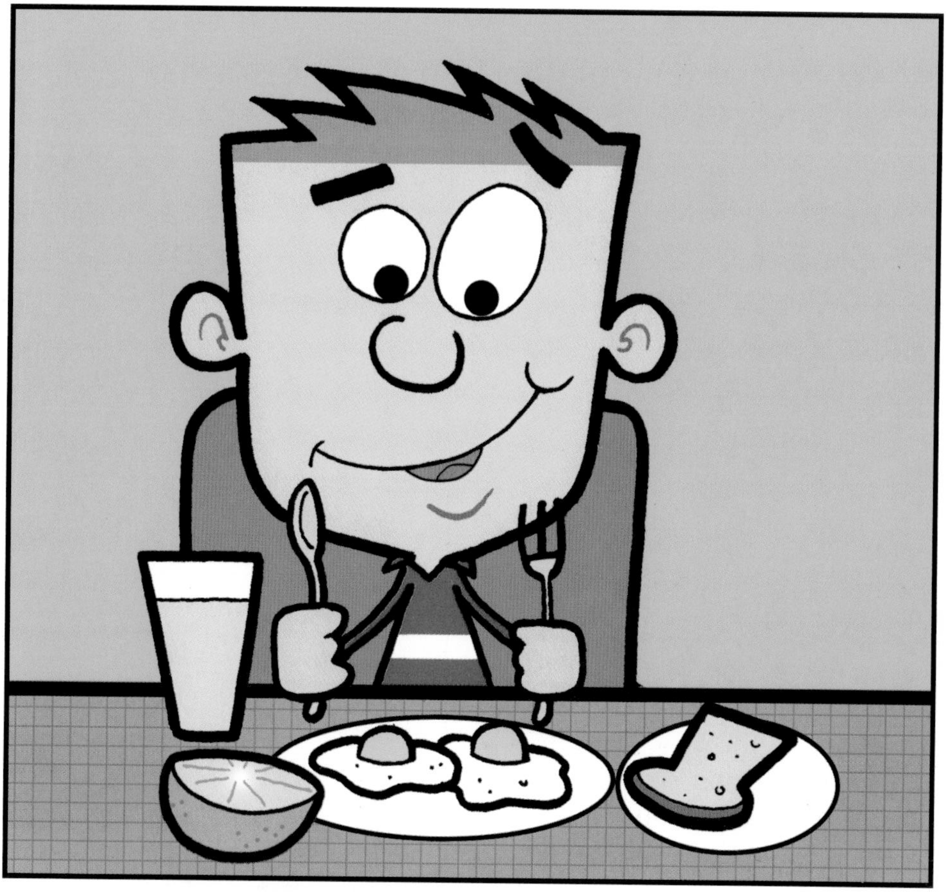

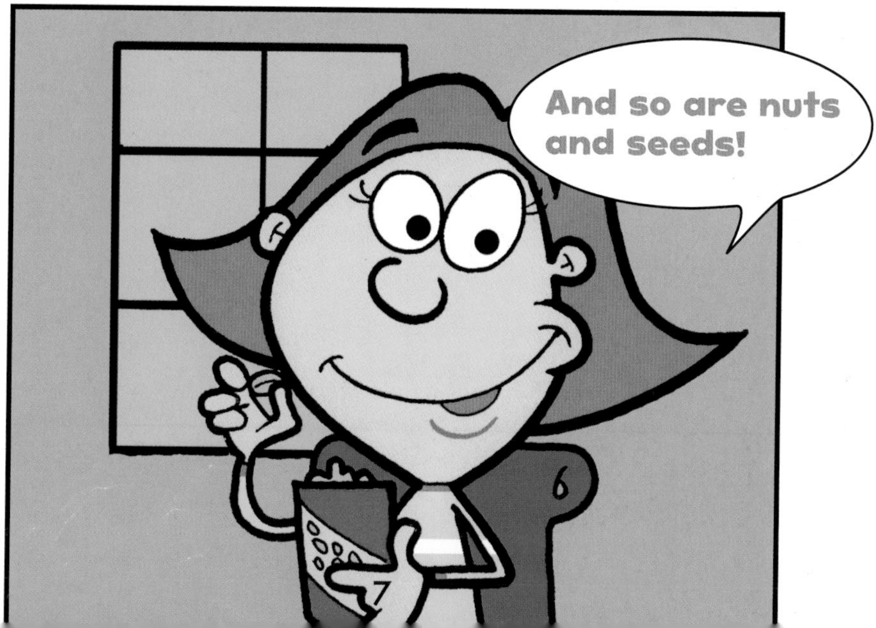
And so are nuts
and seeds!

Where Does It Come From?

Meat comes from animals. Most meat you buy is raised on farms.

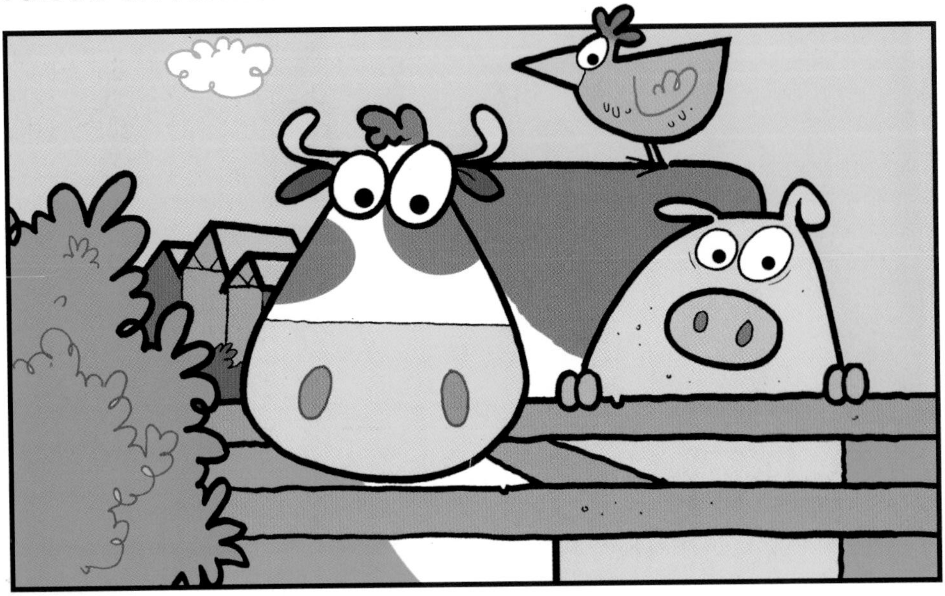

Low-fat meats are best for your body.

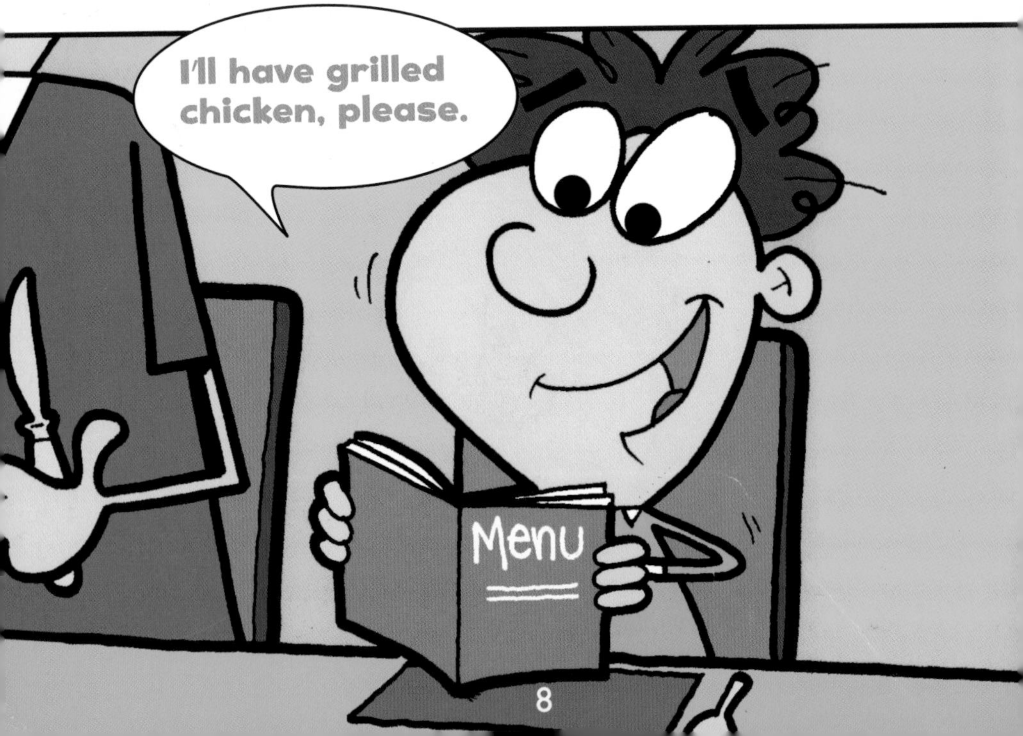
I'll have grilled chicken, please.
Menu

Beef comes from cattle.

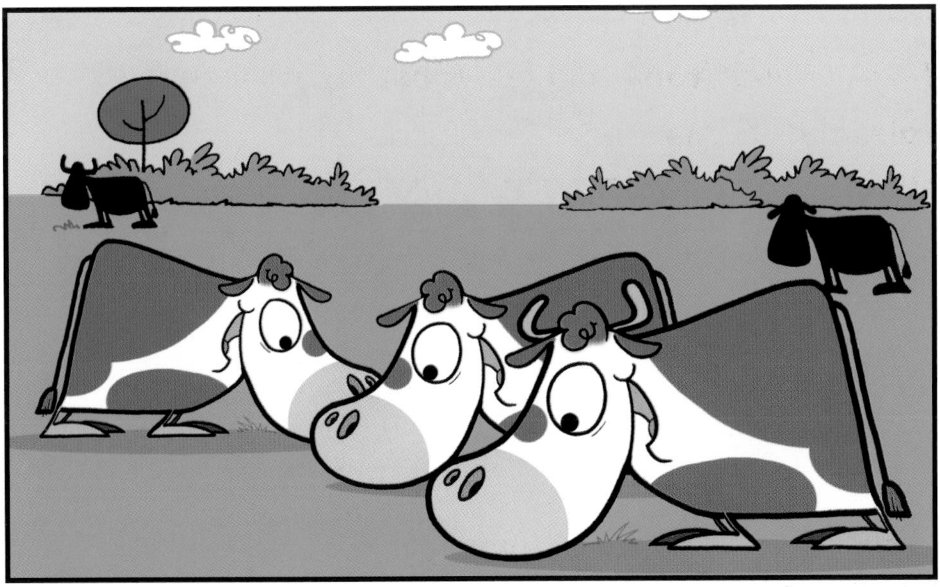

You can choose from steaks, roasts, and ground beef.

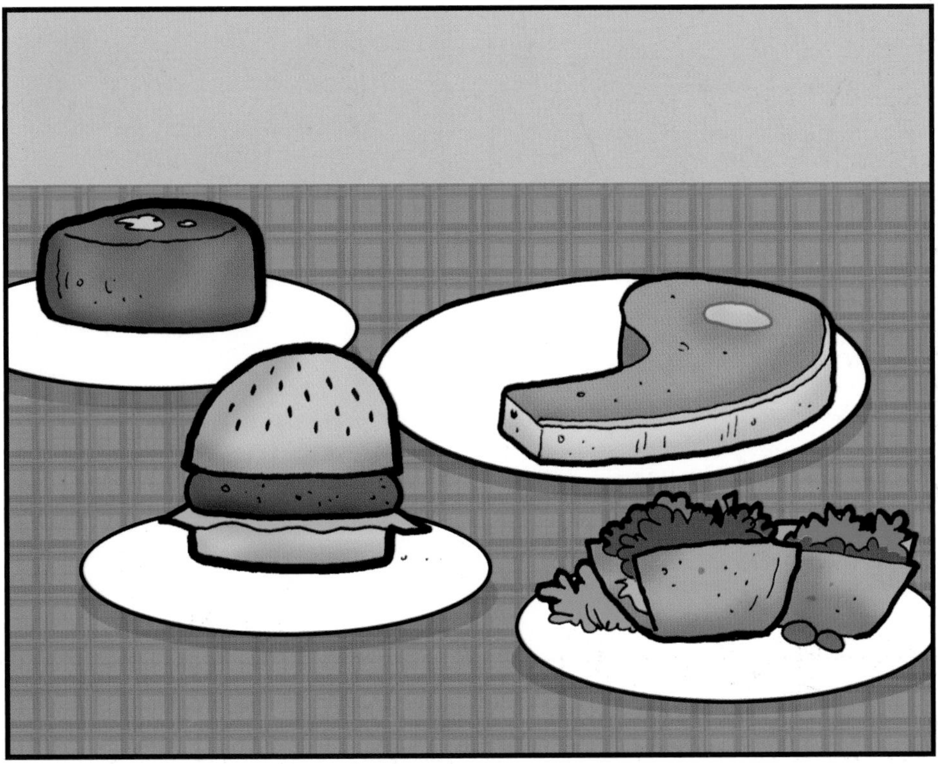

Pork comes from pigs.

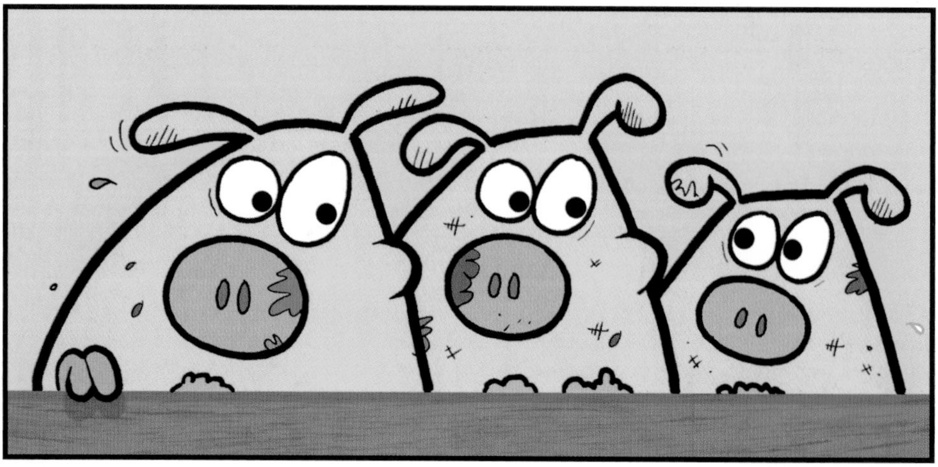

Pork chops and ham are types of pork.

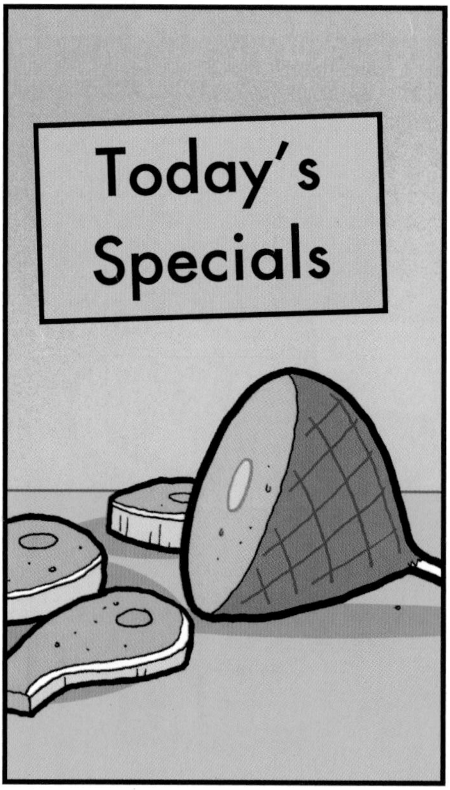
Today's Specials

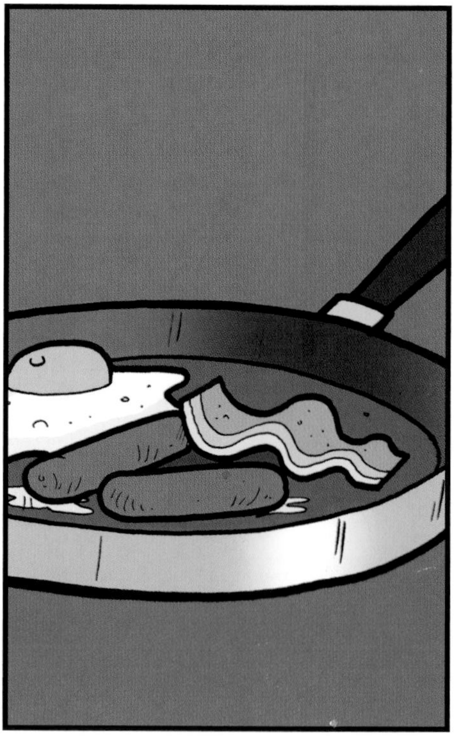

Some sausage and bacon are also made from pork.

Birds raised for food, such as chickens and turkeys, are called poultry.

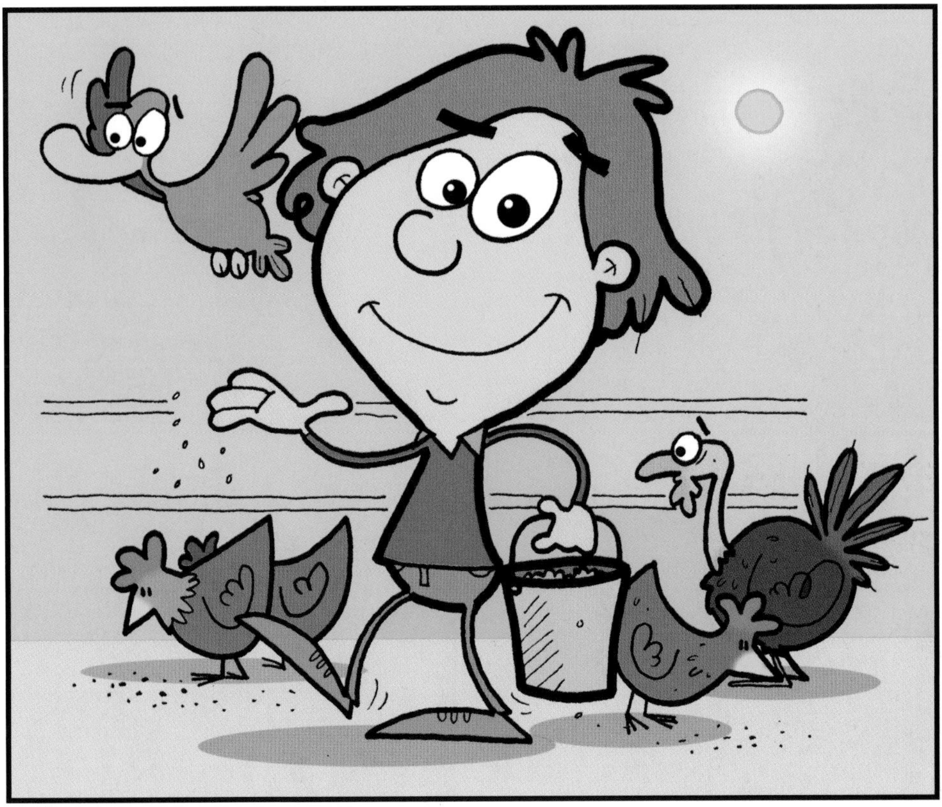

Chickens also lay eggs.

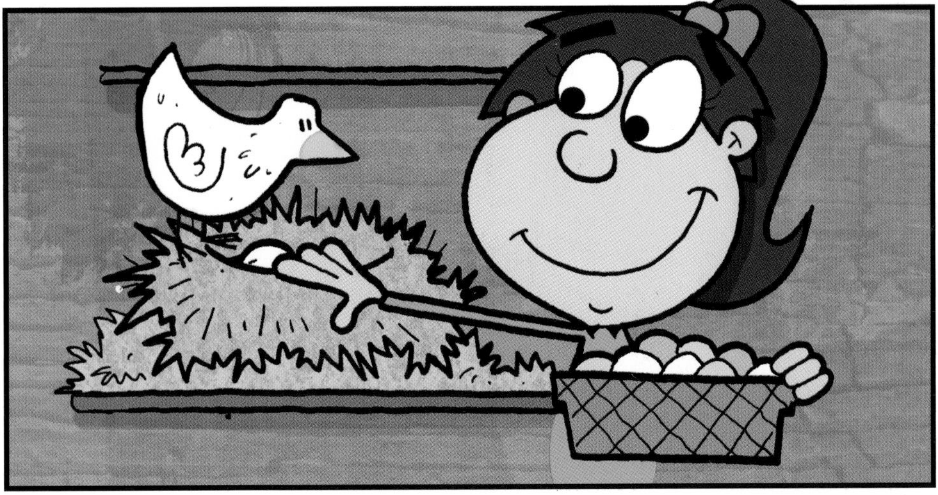

Many people catch their own fish to eat.

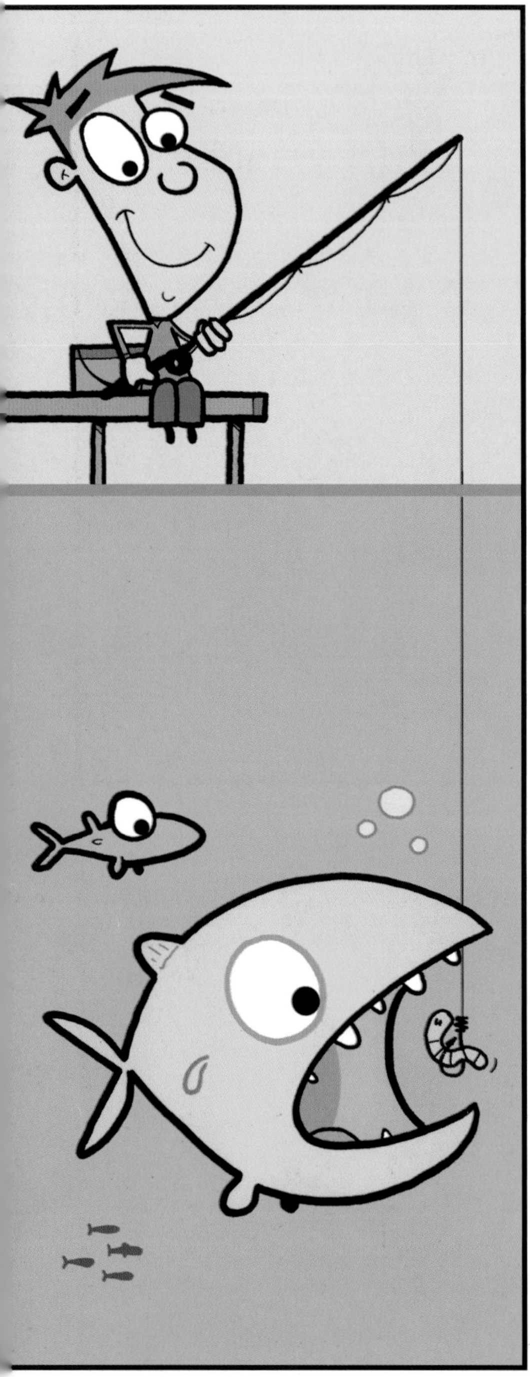

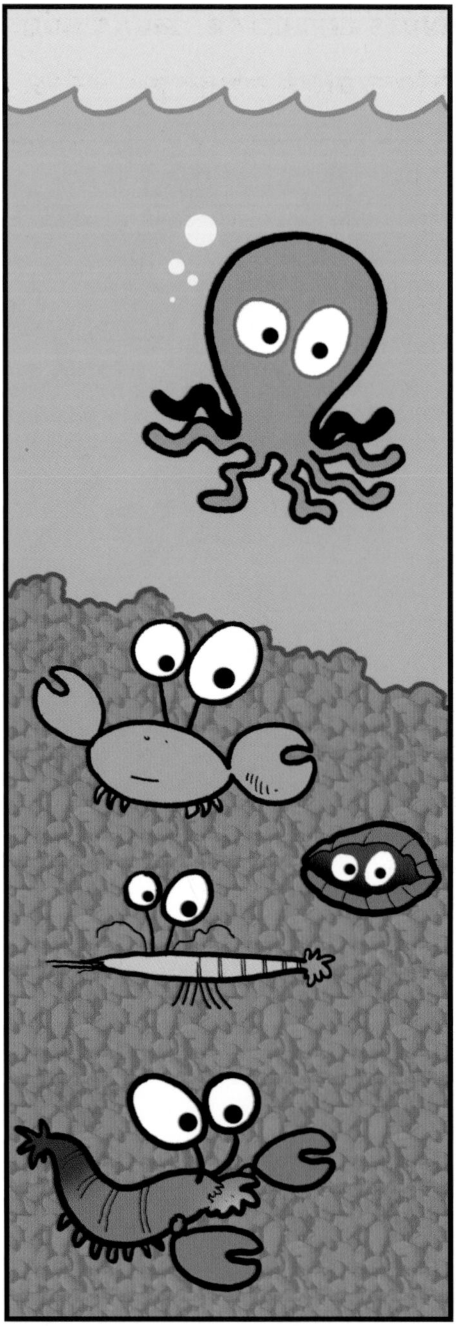

Shellfish and other seafood come from the ocean.

Nuts are large seeds with hard shells.
Most nuts grow on trees.

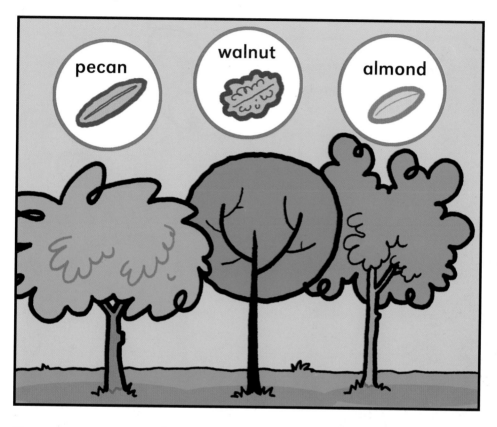

Peanuts grow underground.

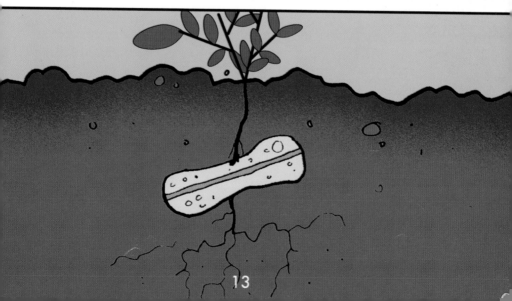

Beans and peas grow in gardens and on farms.

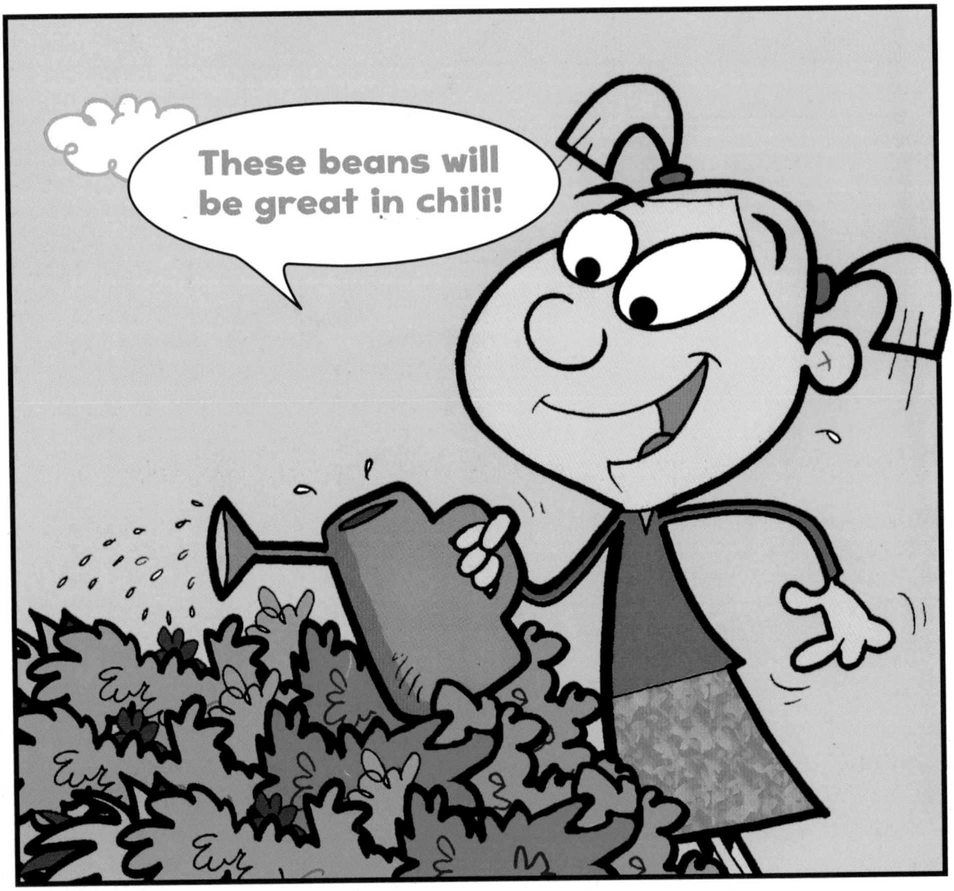
These beans will
be great in chili!

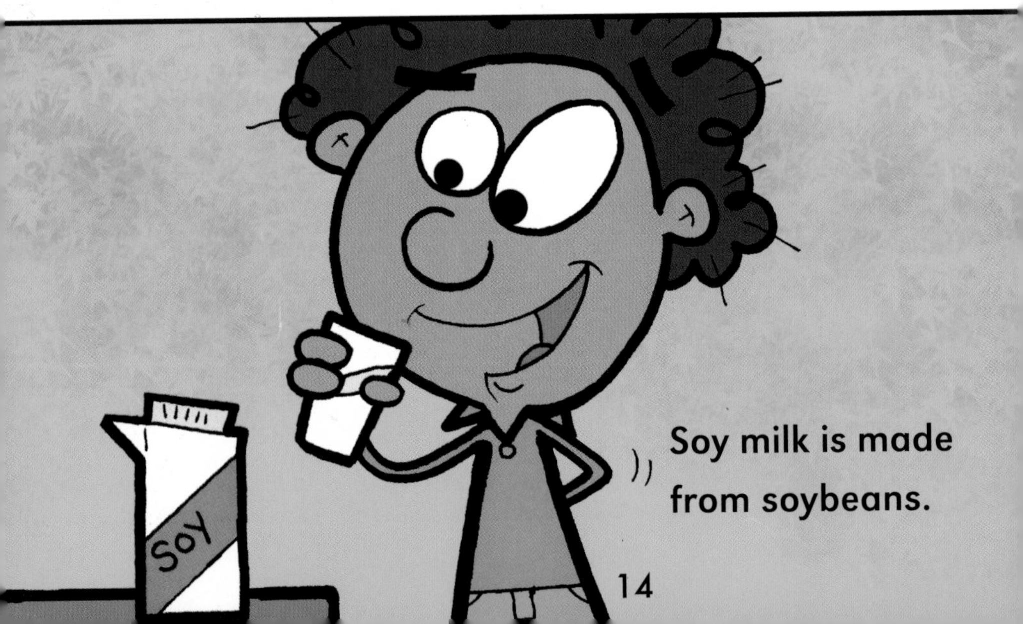
SOY

Soy milk is made from soybeans.

Tofu is made from soy milk.

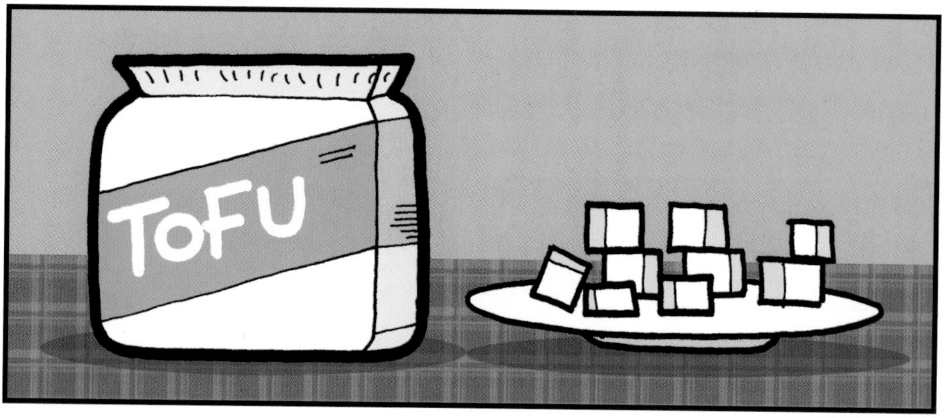
TOFU

Tofu can be used in many dishes instead of meat.

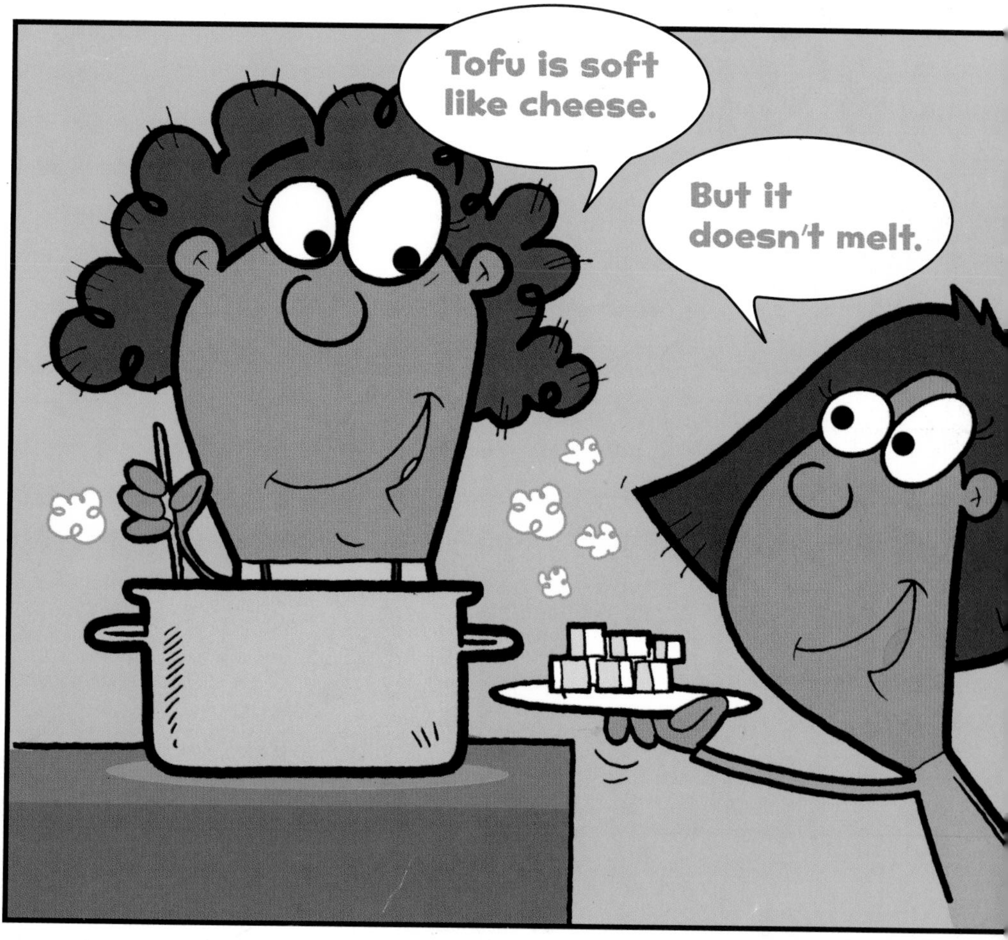
Tofu is soft like cheese.
But it doesn't melt.

Healthy Eating

Your body needs a variety of protein foods every day.

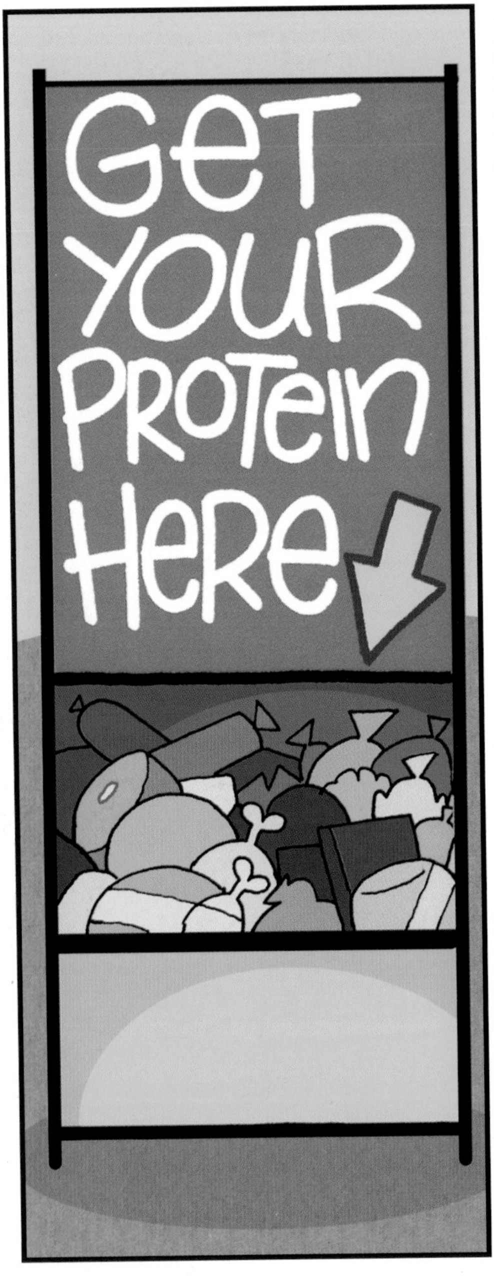
GET YOUR PROTEIN HERE

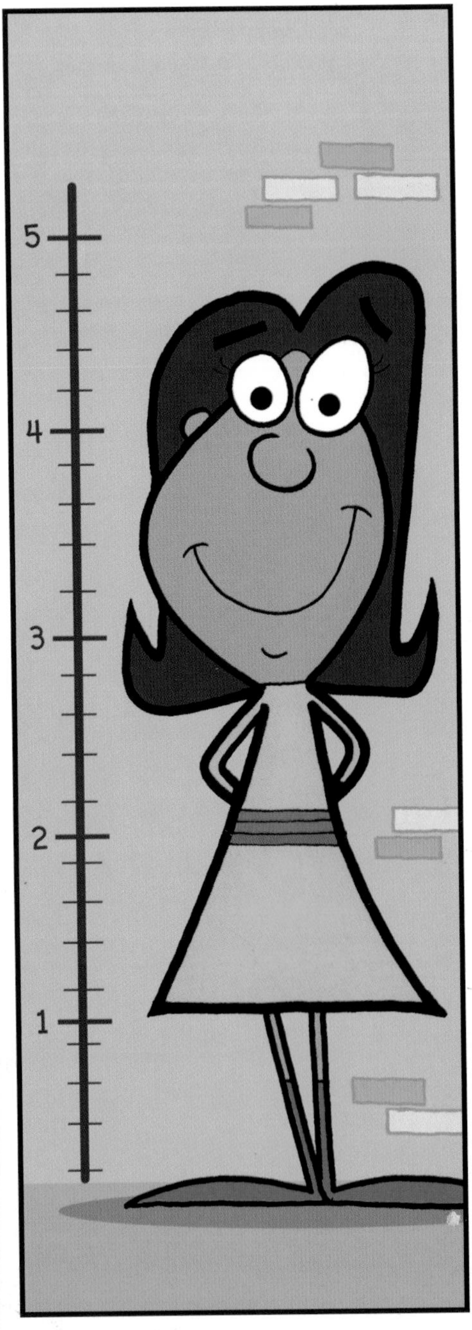
5
4
3
2
1

Protein helps you grow.

Your body uses protein to build and repair muscles.

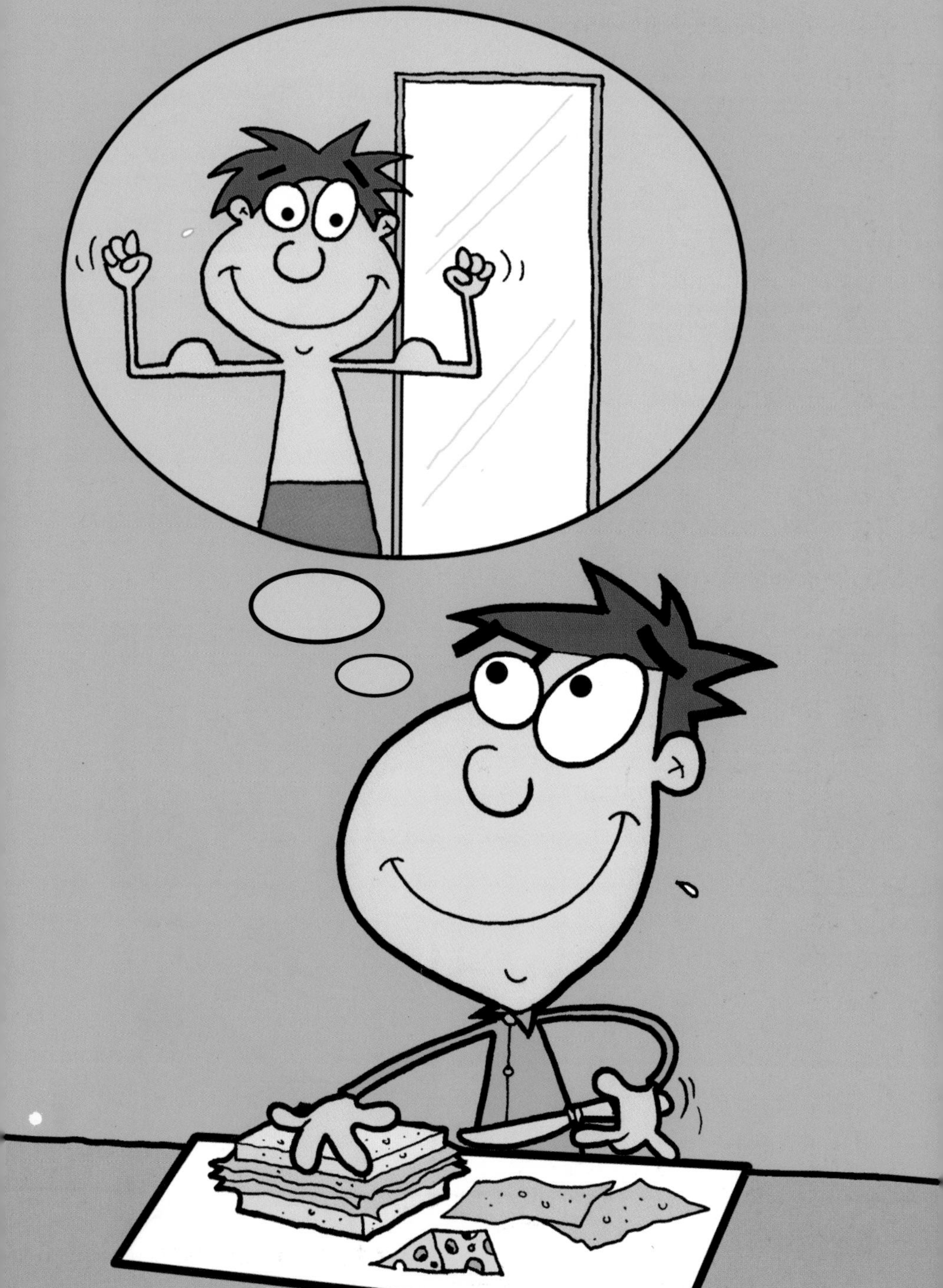

Vegetarians get protein from dried beans, eggs, and nuts instead of meat.

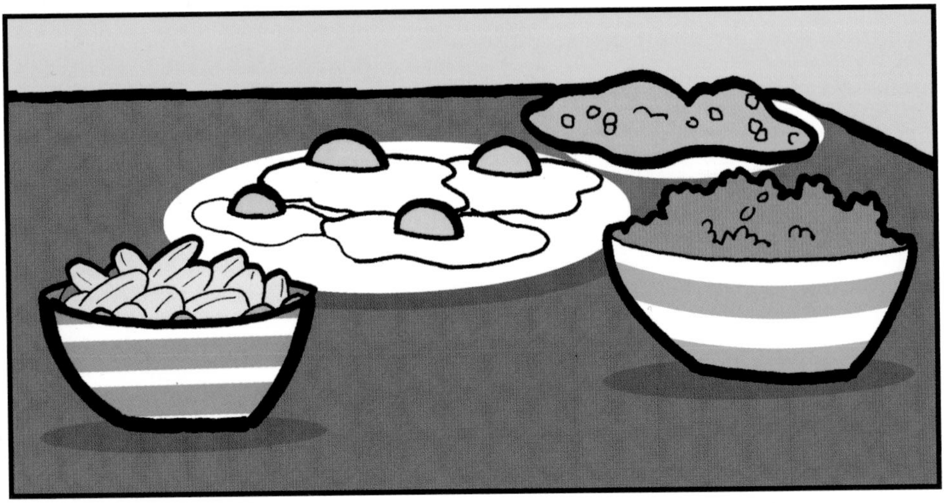

Tofu is another good source of protein that doesn't come from meat.

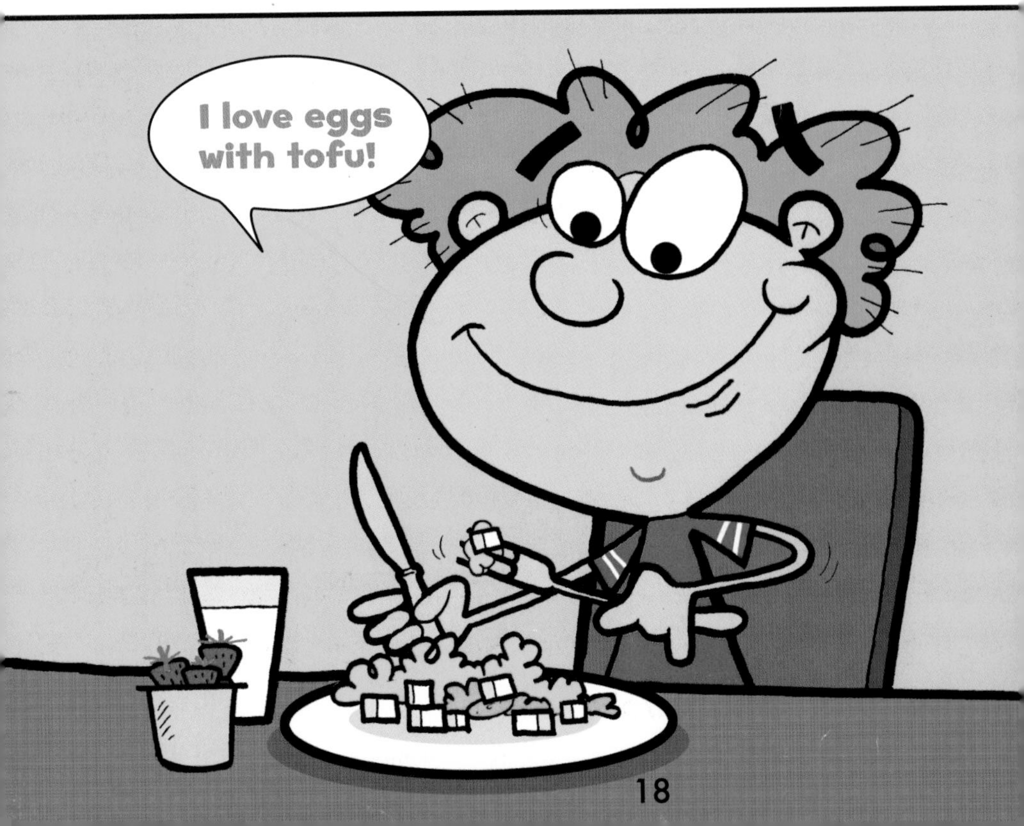
I love eggs with tofu!

Protein foods also give you iron.

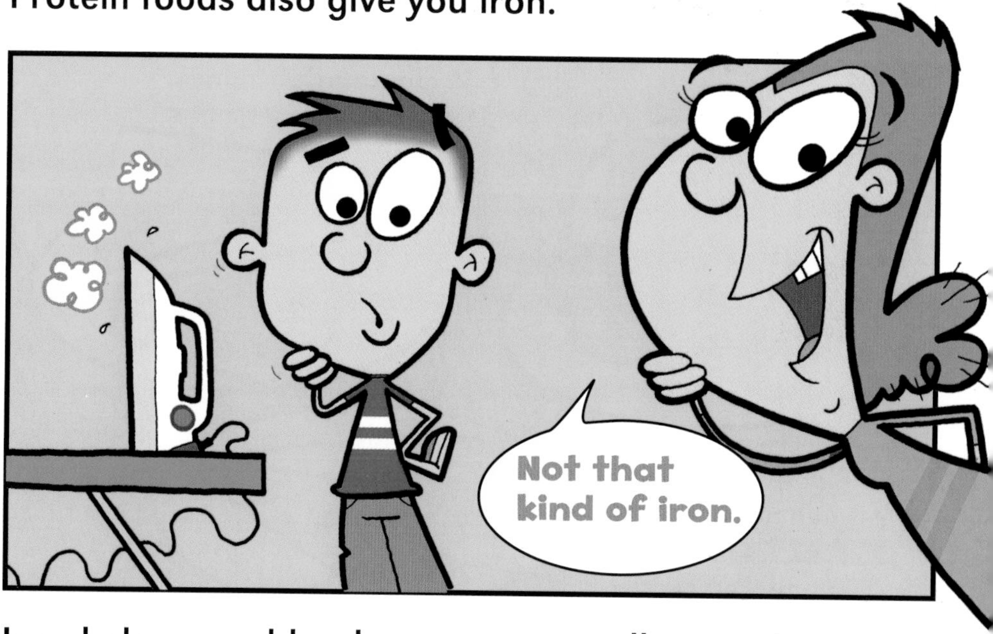
Not that
kind of iron.

Iron helps your blood carry oxygen all around your body.

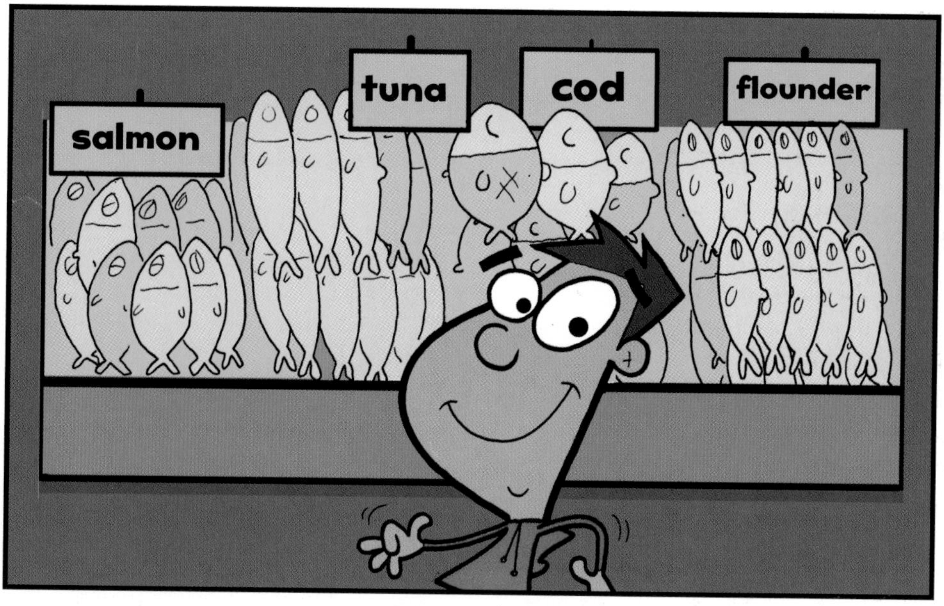
salmon
tuna
cod
flounder

Fish gives you omega-3. This healthy fat is good for your heart and brain.

Kids need four ounces of protein foods each day.

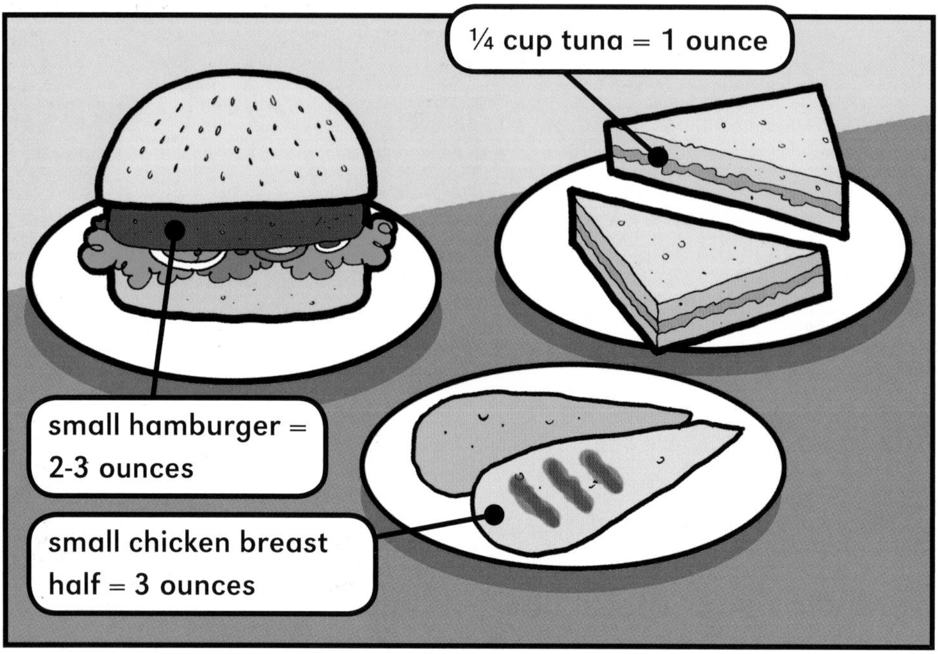
¼ cup tuna = 1 ounce
small hamburger = 2-3 ounces
small chicken breast half = 3 ounces

It's easy to get a serving of protein with meals.

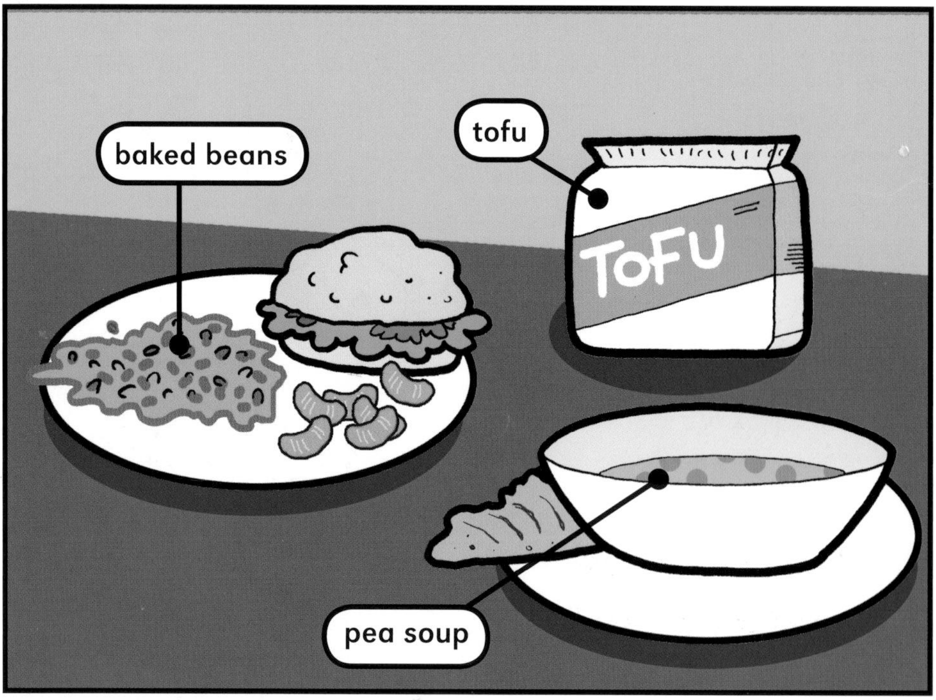
baked beans
tofu
TOFU
pea soup

Protein makes a great snack too!

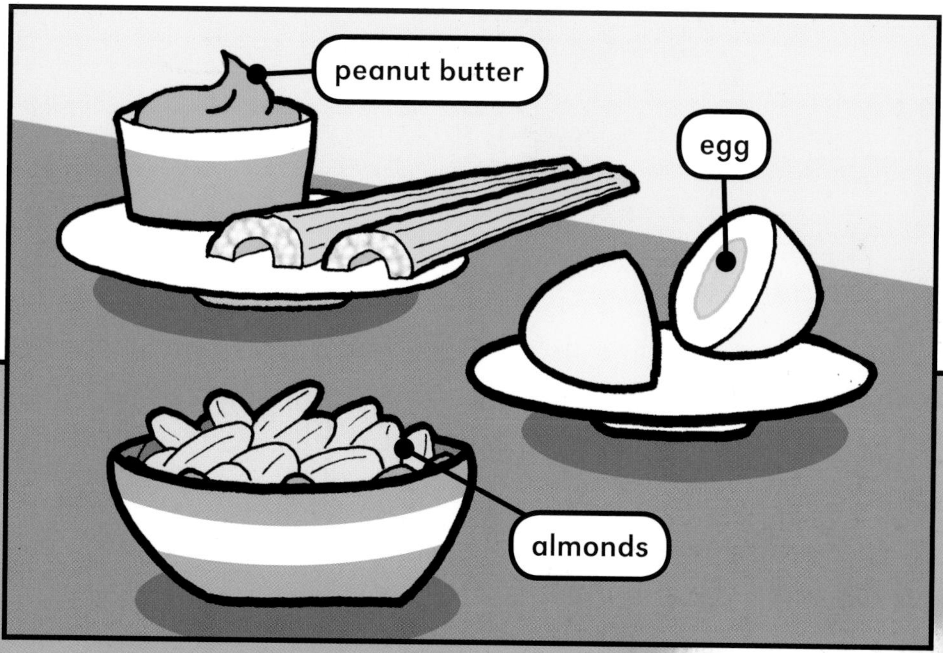
peanut butter
egg
almonds

Following the MyPlate guide helps keep you healthy.

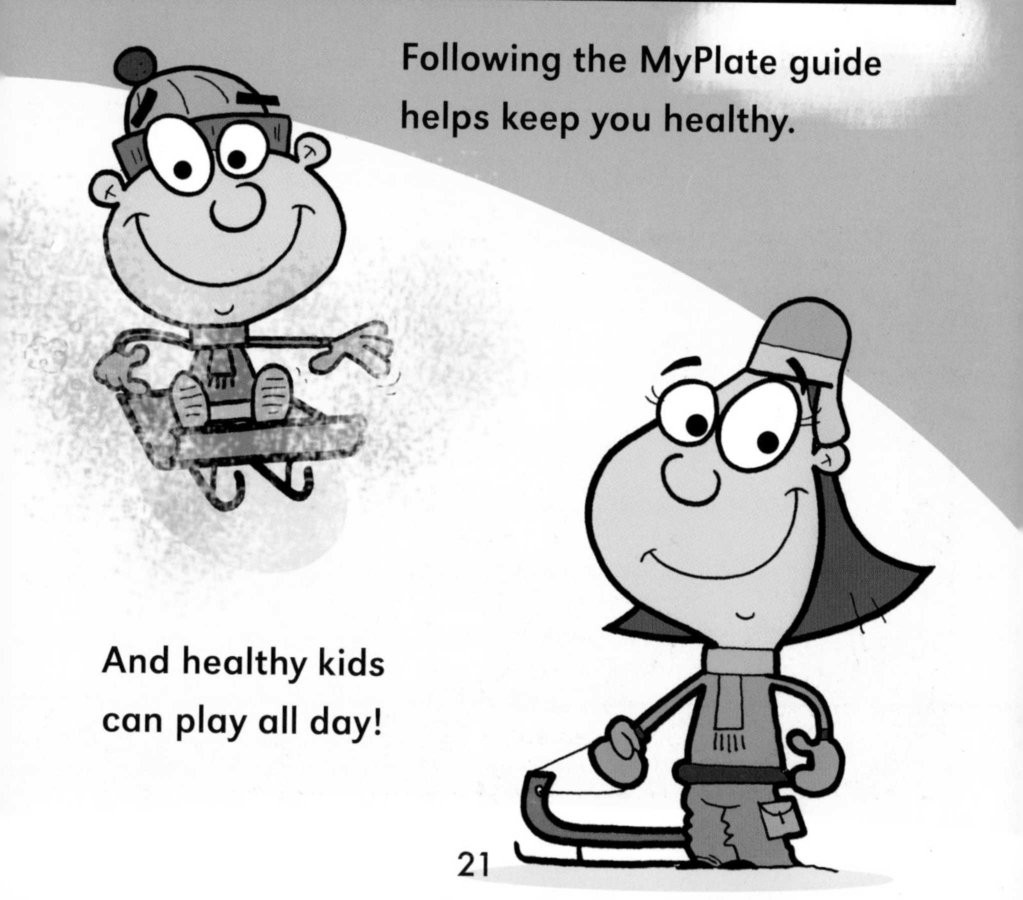

And healthy kids can play all day!

Glossary

cattle—animals raised for dairy products or beef

iron—the mineral in blood that carries oxygen to cells

MyPlate—an illustrated guide that explains healthy eating and shows what a balanced meal should look like

oxygen—a colorless gas that people breathe; humans and animals need oxygen to live

protein—a substance found in foods such as meat, cheese, milk, eggs, and fish

serving—a recommended amount of food or drink

tofu—a soft cheeselike food made from soybeans

vegetarian—someone who does not eat meat

Read More

Adams, Julia. *Proteins.* Good Food. New York: PowerKids Press, 2011.

Burstein, John. *Marvelous Meats and More.* Slim Goodbody's Nutrition Edition. New York: Crabtree Pub., 2010.

Tourville, Amanda Doering. *Fuel the Body: Eating Well.* How to be Healthy! Minneapolis: Picture Window Books, 2009.

Internet Sites

FactHound offers a safe, fun way to find Internet sites related to this book. All of the sites on FactHound have been researched by our staff.

Here's all you do:

Visit *www.facthound.com*

Type in this code: 9781429660914

Super-cool stuff! Check out projects, games and lots more at **www.capstonekids.com**

Index

MyPlate and Healthy Eating

TITLES IN THIS SET:

The Delicious Dairy Group

The Fantastic Fruit Group

The Great Grains Group

Healthy Snacks, Healthy You!

The Incredible Vegetable Group

The Powerful Protein Group

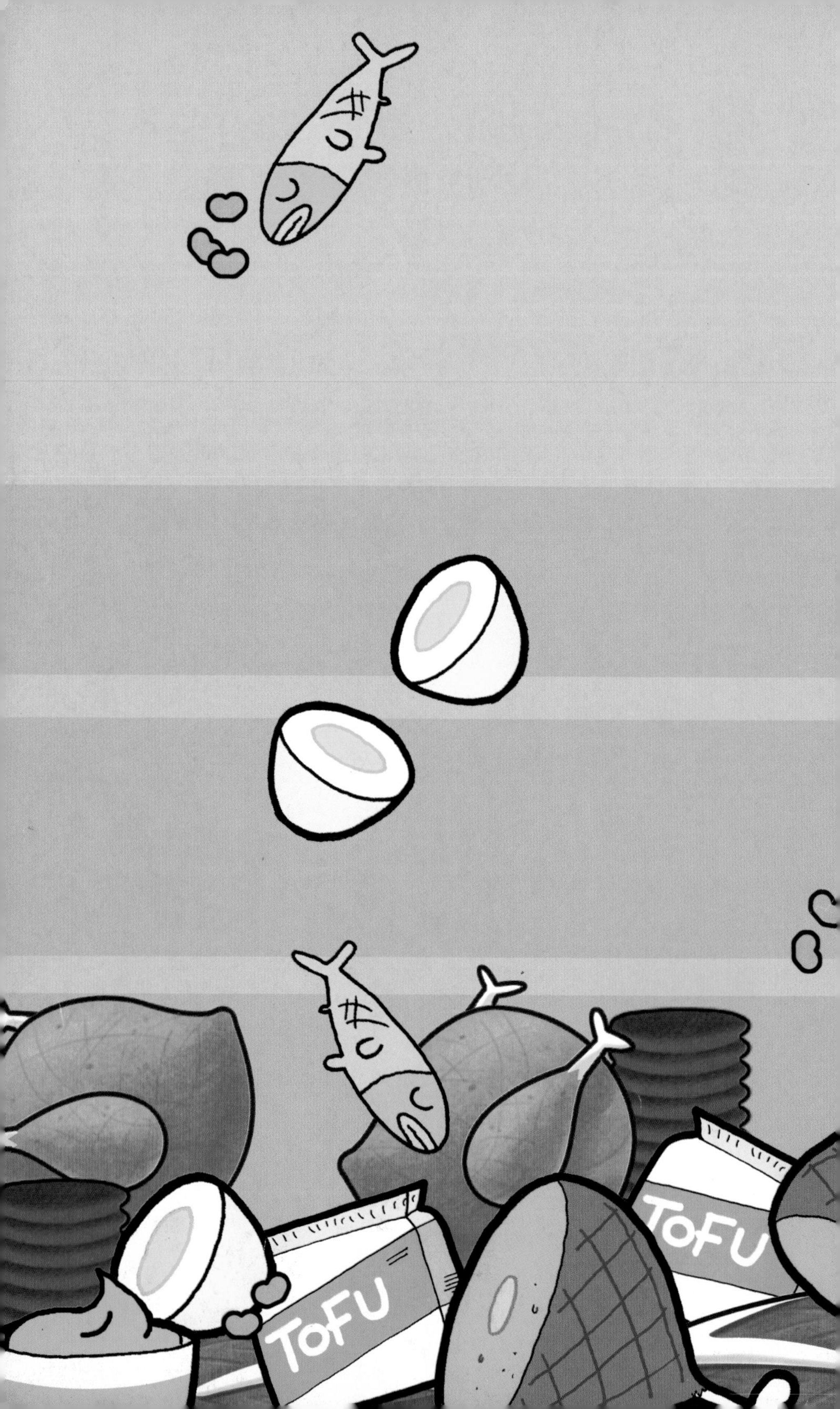
ToFU
ToFU

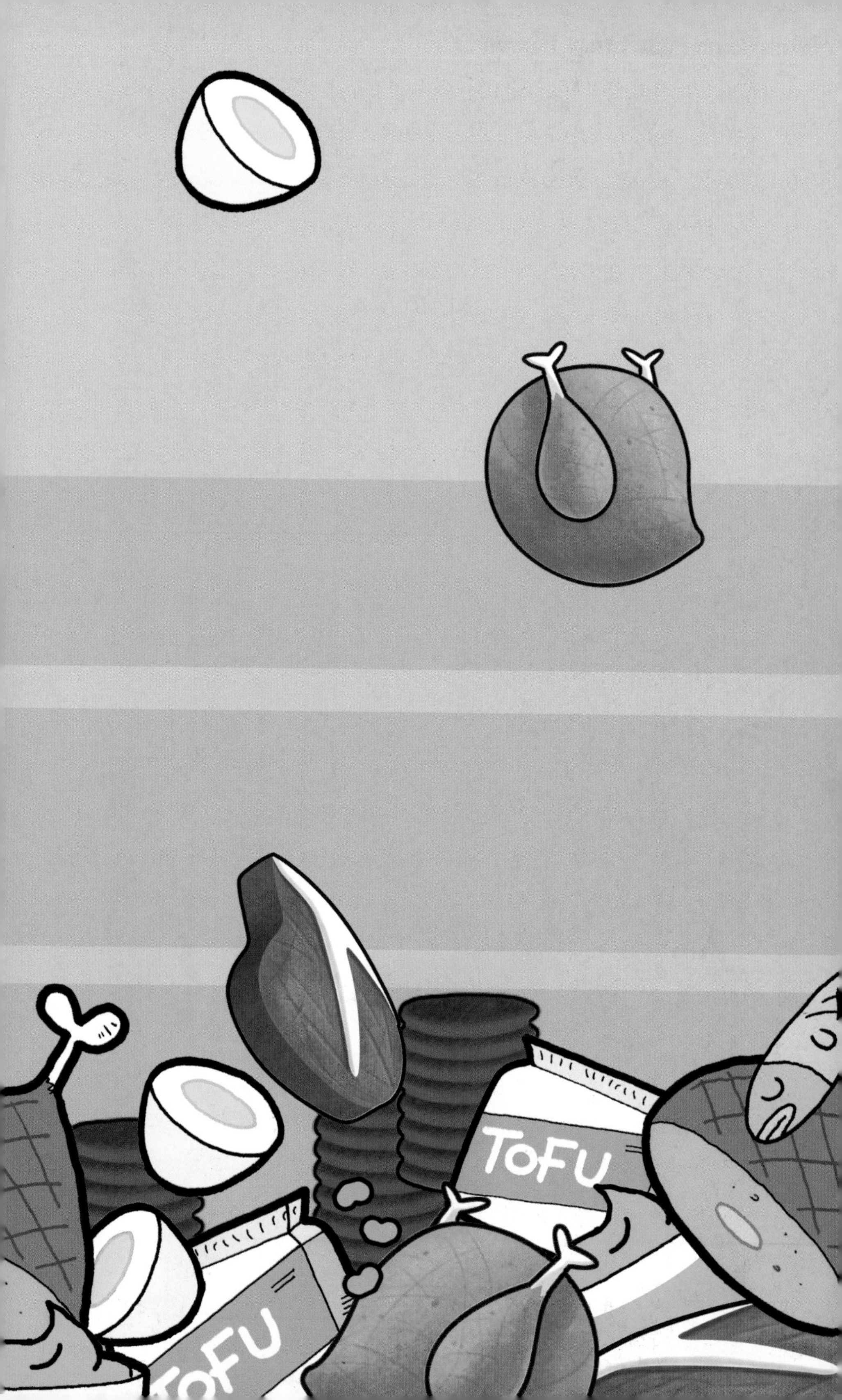
ToFU
ToFU

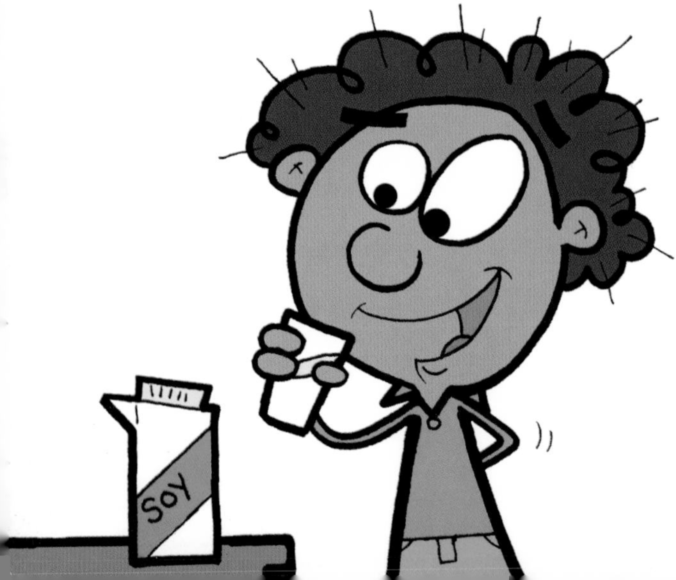
Soy